The Surprising Case of Rachel Baker, Who Prays and Preaches in Her Sleep
by Charles Mais

Address:
HardPress
8345 NW 66TH ST #2561
MIAMI FL 33166-2626
USA
Email: info@hardpress.net

Elton Mayo.

THE

SURPRISING CASE

OF

RACHEL BAKER,

WHO PRAYS AND PREACHES IN HER SLEEP:

WITH SPECIMENS OF HER EXTRAORDINARY PERFORMAN-
CES TAKEN DOWN ACCURATELY IN SHORT HAND AT
THE TIME; AND SHOWING THE UNPARALLELED
POWERS SHE POSSESSES TO PRAY, EXHORT,
AND ANSWER QUESTIONS, DURING
HER UNCONSCIOUS STATE.

*The whole authenticated by the most respectable testi-
mony of living witnesses.*

BY CHARLES MAIS,

OF THE CITY OF NEW-YORK, STENOGRAPHER.

Tell me the visions of my dream that I have seen, and the interpretation thereof.
Nebuchadnezzar to Belteshazzar. Dan. 4. 9.

NEW-YORK:

PRINTED BY MARKS, 63 ANTHONY-STREET.

......

1814,

DISTRICT OF NEW-YORK, ss.

Be it remembered, that on the sixteenth day of November, in the thirty-ninth year of the Independence of the United States of America, Charles Mais, of the said District, has deposited in this office the title of a book, the right whereof he claims as author, in the words and figures following, to wit:

The surprising case of Rachel Baker, who prays and preaches in her sleep; with specimens of her extraordinary performances taken down accurately in short hand at the time; and showing the unparalleled powers she possesses to pray, exhort, and answer questions during her unconscious state. The whole authenticated by the most respectable testimony of living witnesses, by Charles Mais, of the city of New-York, Stenographer.

Tell me the vision of my dream, that I have seen, and the interpretation thereof.
Nebuchadnezzar to Belteshazzar. Dan. 4. 9.

In conformity to the act of the congress of the United States, entitled "An Act for the encouragement of Learning, by securing the copies of Maps, Charts, and Books to the authors and proprietors of such copies, during the time therein mentioned." And also to an act, entitled "An Act, supplementary to an Act, entitled an Act for the encouragement of Learning, by securing the copies of Maps, Charts, and Books to the authors and proprietors of such copies, during the times therein mentioned, and extending the benefits thereof to the arts of designing, engraving, and etching historical and other prints."

THERON RUDD,
Clerk of the Southern District of New-York.

TO DOCTORS

MITCHILL, DOUGLASS, BIRCH, MOTT, AND BRUCE.

GENTLEMEN,

HAVING had an invitation to witness one of the periodical exercises of Miss RACHEL BAKER, during her stay in this city, I used the opportunity, to take in short hand, what she delivered.

Repeated applications have been made to me, to transcribe, and communicate to the public what I wrote, with such medical history and opinion as could he obtained from the gentlemen of the Faculty who had been consulted on her case.

I understand, that a statement of the case, was read before some members of the Literary and Philosophical Society, and of the College of Physicians and Surgeons. I take the liberty of soliciting that paper, or any other which you may furnish, to give additional interest to what I have already prepared for the press.

Your respectable names are of sufficient importance to apologise for my intreaty; but gentlemen, you are aware that the public feeling is excited, and that amidst the suggestions of fancy, the perplexities of doubt, and the insiduous whispers of slander, some guide is necessary to conduct the general judgment. From whence shall this aid be derived, but from the opinions of gentlemen possessing your medical skill and critical acumen? your knowledge of the case, derived from frequent observation, enables you to gratify the public curiosity.

I beg you to excuse this request of an individual, who, though unknown to you, antisipates from your general courtesy, a favourable issue, and subscribes himself   most respectfully
                    gentlemen,
                    your humble servant,
                        C. MAIS,

New-York, 12th Nov. 1814.

New-York, 14th Nov. 1814.

Mr. Charles Mais,

Sir,

In compliance with your request, we enclose you a memorandum of the remarkable case you mentioned; as noted by Doctor Mitchill. We have examined this statement, and are satisfied of its accuracy. The facts and opinions therein contained, will form a basis for the publication you meditate to make. To render this more instructive and satisfactory, we also forward some of the questions put and answers received during her exercises, which, in our judgment, form a capital illustration of the subject.

We have the honour to be,

Sir, your obedient servants,

JOHN H. DOUGLASS.
JOSHUA E. R. BIRCH.
VALENTINE MOTT.
ARCHIBALD BRUCE.

Minutes made by SAMUEL L. MITCHILL, M. D. and P.
on the case of a young woman whose internal sen-
ses, and organs of speech, are strangely affected,
at certain times, when she is not awake.

———————————————

IN yielding to the request of my learned friends to
submit to their disposal my sketch of the singular case
upon which we were lately consulted, I hope I shall
not only gratify their laudable curiosity, but furnish
some interesting materials towards a theory of the
delicate and complicated operations, of the human
mind.

Rachel Baker about twenty years old, experienced
at the age of fourteen some religious concern, and in
consequence thereof joined the Presbyterian Church
in the county Onondaga New York. Becoming un-
easy about two years afterwards she underwent a religious submersion and became a member of the Baptist church. To that society she has ever since been
united.

She is possessed of a constitution naturally good
and it has never been materially impaired by disease.
Since her connection with the latter society, she has
been in a devout frame of mind, but never inclined to
superstition on the one part, nor to enthusiasm on the
other. Her deportment is sedate, reserved, and diffident. Being little prone to talk, she seldom commences a conversation, and even when spoken to is
not fond of indulging in discourse. She has been in
the habit of frequenting religious meetings, but in no
other manner than the regular members of the society
to which she belongs. Her moral character is fair
and exemplary.

Nevertheless, her faculties have been called into
action after an uncommon manner. Once a day for
about three years, or from the time of her second bap-
tism she has suffered a paroxism which usually con-
tiues an hour. It sometimes ends in forty five minutes, and then again is prolonged an hour and a quar-

ter. The fit invades her at nine o'clock in the evening or about ordinary bed time. It commences with spasmodic agitation, heaviness of respiration, and anxiety, but differs from fevers of the intermittent type, in having neither a cold, a hot, nor a sweating stage.

The intermittent disorder which Miss Baker suffers, seizes her in bed or in her chair if she sits up. After a few moments of torpor or somnolency, at the usual hour she loses her consciousness and begins to speak in an audible and frequently a forcible tone. She is usually found lying in a supine posture and so free from all voluntary action save that of her organs of speech, and a little inclination of her neck, that she stirs neither hand nor foot from the beginning to the termination of the attack. Except the lips, throat, and neighbouring parts there is no more action discoverable in her than if she was totally disabled by palsy. She may be literally said to lie still. Thus this modest damsel falls into a devotional exercise as soon as she loses her consciousness. It would be improper to consider her asleep tho' her body and limbs are so quiet and her eyes steadily closed.

The exercise consists of three parts : the first an incipient or opening prayer to God, similar to those of our reformed preachers ; the second an addres or exhortation as to a human audience present, and listening to her ; and the third a closing supplication to the Supreme being resembling in its principal points the final offering of confession and thanksgiving from the pulpit. She neither sings nor selects a text, but occasionally recites verses from the hymns of Watts.

It has been remarked that the topics of these exercises are strictly conformable to the Calvinistic faith. In them she manifests an extensive acquaintance with the doctrinal parts of the scriptures, and readily cites the several books. · Some have supposed that she dwells more upon the Evangelists than upon the historical prophetical or epistolary writings. Others however are of a different opinion, observing that she quotes freely from all. Her language is usually plain but sometimes ornamental and figurative; her articulation distinct and occasionally earnest and impressive. Her sentiments are biblical and conformable to the orthodox protestantism of her sect. Her opinions delivered during the paroxism, and I meddle with no other, are as sensible, intelligent and indicative of thought as you generally hear. The purity of her expressions has been noticed as unexceptionable. She may be accosted during the performance. She hears the words addressed to her, and listens to catch them. But though her attention is thus roused she is not excited to ordinary wakefulness. The queries put to her always provoke replies. The answers are pious, discreet, and indicative of religious meditation. I doubt whether the waking persons present could have responded to the questions I put, more theologically right than this unconscious girl.

Her words are poured forth in a fluent and rapid stream. She rarely appears at a loss for an expression, but proceeds with as much readiness as the greater part of those who pray and preach. At times she is remarkably animated, and gives point to her sentences by the most expressive emphasis. But when the current of her thought is interrupted by a query, the catenation of her discourse is also broken; the original or preceding subject is abandoned and a new train of ideas suggested by the interrogation is substituted. This she pursues as long as she has any thing to offer, and then relapses into her ordinary topics of exhortation. If now a different question be put it immediately gives a new direction to her thoughts, and in her reply she dwells upon it until she has nothing further to observe; after which she again returns to her customary tenor of discourse. In this way I have received' from her, answers in terms devotionally appropriate to half a dozen successive questions on serious subjects.

Her pulse during the exercise was full, equable,

and flowing, without tremor, flutter, or intermission. Both, as to force and frequency it has a good healthy beat. The temperature of her hand, arm, face, and forehead, was so much like that of a person asleep that I could distinguish no preternatural heat or cold in them. There was neither dryness nor moisture upon the skin. However toward the end of the paroxism there was an evident diminution of the arterial pulsation at the wrist. On some occasions the frequency is increased eight strokes in a minute. Her features, which had in no instance indicated the smallest distortion, wore the look of languor and exhaustion. The eyes have been observed to be turned upwards, and their muscles in a tremulous spasm. She is insensible to all the stimuli which it has been thought prudent to apply, for the purpose of rousing her.

At the end of the exercise, she had a few small spasms of the arms and throat. The latter resembled an hysterical inflation of the pharaynx. She was agitated with an emotion between sighing and groaning: And after a turn of restlessness and moaning that lasted from two to fifteen minutes, but without waking, consciousness, or even opening her eyes, she passed from her state of *purturbation* to that of *natural and tranquil sleep.* This continues usually until morning, as is common to persons in good health, when she awakes invigorated and refreshed as if nothing uncommon had happened, and professes herself ignorant of every part of the transaction, with which she becomes acquainted only by information from others. After certain of her prolonged discourses, her hands have been violently clenched, and all the muscles of the trunk and limbs stiffened by spasm for a short time. During the intermission she is as well as other persons, and works diligently with her needle. She considers it as a heavy affliction that she should be the vehicle of devotional effusions which give her neither pleasure nor edification, and which expose her to the animadversion of all who are admitted to behold her.

One of the curious particulars in her case is, the persuasion she possesses that she is wide awake. On one occasion I observed, during her sermon, that she ought to be silent and not talk so long and so loud in her sleep. She heard me and denied that she was asleep. Her eye lids were, as usual, accurately closed, and there was no sign of winking. She declared herself awake, and in confirmation of her opinion, described in vivid and glowing strains the spectacle then bright in her view; consisting of the angels, saints, and souls of just men made perfect, ministering before the throne of the Almighty, clothed in robes white as snow, and without spot or blemish, and looking like fine linen wrought by skilful hands, and with curious and cunning workmanship. Another memorable particular is, that while she is in this paroxysm, she acts under the persuasion that it is the duty of those who are renewed by all merciful grace to direct poor wanderers to the strait way, while at the same time her waking belief is, that it is not apostolical for a woman to be a public teacher of holy things.

To remove this train of symptoms, her physicians had attempted to abate the excitement of her sensorium by blood-letting. This, though practised to a degree considerably debilitating, did not prevent the paroxysm, nor break the habit of recurrence. Recourse was also had to opiates, with the intention of composing her to sleep, but their anodyne qualities were of no avail. The fit was not broken, and the diseased associations went on as before. I have not learned that any other important remedies were tried.

She was brought to New York in October, 1814, to procure medical counsel, to try the effect of traveling, and to experience the influence of a maritime atmosphere. Doctor Douglass was requested to take charge of her health; and by that gentleman I was desired to visit her. It was concluded, through tenderness, to forbear all recommendation of active pre-

B

scriptions, until her case could be satisfactorily observed. When thereafter, a plan of treatment should be formed, it might, at any future day be communicated. Afterwards Dr. Birch, Dr. Mott, and Dr. Bruce were invited to a consultation on her case, and they also consented to postpone for the present, all interference by remedies.

The journey did not suspend the accustomed visitations. The taverns where she stopped were witnesses of her involuntary prayers and exhortations. Nor did the air of the ocean produce any salutary effect. In the city she obtained no respite; every evening her fit was renewed. Now and then there seemed to be an increase of its violence. For if there was any memorable alteration, it continued longer and was followed by severer spasms and greater debility. This might possibly be caused by the multitudes who crouded into her chamber to learn for themselves. Curiosity was so strong, that, on the day of her departure, many persons followed her out of town to the place of resting until the morn, that they might witness the spectacle, not of a waking preacher and a drowsy audience, but of a preacher abstracted from outward things, holding forth to a wondering and staring company.

After this recital of her case, there will be no need of considering with some persons that it is an example of supernatural agency; nor of supposing with others that it is an instance of refined imposture. It is capable of solution upon medical principles, and of being referred by their aid to its proper place in the animal economy.

It differs from sleep by the performance of hearing, of attention, of speaking and of acting in a manner that evinces a remarkable degree of method and consistency. There is no feverish condition of her system to countenance the supposition of its being Delirium. Still less is it the moping of melancholy or the raving of mania.

In some of its forms, it manifests its nearness to

hysteria and catalepsy. It resembles reverie ; though this is so moderate in the present case, that the train of thought may be changed by interrogatories, without rousing her. It is allied to somnambulism ; though she remains in a decumbent posture with her eye-lids constantly shut. It would not be incorrect to liken it to the common though, curious phenomena of dreaming. Strictly its name is Somniloquism ; at least as far as speaking goes. The actual condition of her faculties has such an affinity to reverie, somnambulism and dreaming, as to induce a conviction that it is a kindred malady, or an affection of the bodily and mental powers nearly associated with them, or with one or more of the other diseases mentioned in this paragraph.

It is reported that the habitation of the patient's father was frequently opened to travelling preachers, from the days of her childhood to the commencement of her present malady. With a constitution readily susceptible of religious impressions, and a correct and retentive memory, she appears to have treasured up a large proportion of the words and phrases uttered in her presence by her spiritual teachers. She can read ; but not with ease, or freedom. It may therefore be presumed that her ideas were derived in a great measure from the public exhibitions; and that they have been continued and renewed by constant applications. While these impressions were deepest, the age of puberty arrived, a period when the female frame acquires additional sensibilities, and undergoes a peculiar revolution. For a while she doubted whether she had any participation in the great work of redemption. During this period her parents remarked that her exercises were gloomy and desponding. At length she received consolation; and her nightly performances immediately became sprightly and cheerful. The love of her Maker was now quickened into a lively emotion; and her desire to be near him was followed by an admission into the society of his adorers. The attendance on worship,

which with most children is an affair of obedience or
imitation, was now become in her a matter of desire
and duty.

Her docile and susceptible mind has undoubtedly
been moulded and conformed by the power of habit.
She has acquired modes of thinking and of acting
which recur at periodical times ; and like some other
diseases, without either volition or consciousness. If
the paroxysm be compared to those of the hysteric, or
as some pathologists may suppose of the epileptic
kind ; like them it effaces all knowledge of herself,
and recollection of occurrences during the fit. In
this state, she possesses a distinct recollection of all
her religious information. She goes further. She
exercises the faculty of invention, by combining her
ideas in new ways, by pronouncing discourses infi-
nitely diversified amidst the sameness of topics, and
of uttering some phrases and metaphors that are peculiar to herself. And yet she forgets that she ever
exerted this recollection, or made any use of her in-
ventive powers. The condition of her sensorium is
such, that devotional trains of thinking are presented
to her, and she gives utterance to them in words. In
the main, they are very similar to those she has been
accustomed to hear. From these they differ about
as much as glowing and connected dreams vary from
waking thoughts. These images never would offer
themselves during her wakeful state, on account of
the occupation of her mind and body in other pursuits.
But when the will ceases to preside, the latent impressions gain a temporary ascendancy, run their
round and disappear.

Perhaps, the most extraordinary trait in her case,
is the readiness and aptness with which she answers
the questions by which the bye-standers interrupt the
current of her thoughts. On the principal part of
these however, there may be observed a profound
submission of every thing to the disposal and govern-
ment of the Most High; without entering into moral,
political, or economical details. Such general re-

plies of humility and reverence are the easiest of all
to give, and are of no particular or individual appli-
cation when analyzed. They are in their matter and
composition remarkably similar, in this respect, to
the exercises when they proceed without interruption.
They have a strong tincture of the same quality.

To comprehend the present case, let a few facts
be stated, not from the books of metaphysics or medicine, but from real life.

A young woman is now living, who has been
known to feel a most imperative call to go forth and
preach to her neighbours and acquaintance. It has
happened, that on these occasions, the missionary
has suffered strong and regular hysteria. After a
few days, the paroxysm usually abates, she gets well
and loses the inclination and ability to be a minister
of the word. She has experienced about a dozen of
such fits of religious hysterics.

A layman who is accustomed to attend regularly
the worship of a christian society, has acquired the
habit of rising from bed and of praying and preaching
during his sleep. This man is a steady, moderate,
and respectable attendant; but has never experienced
the call, of conversion. His exercises are consonant
to those he has been accustomed to hear. He is
wholly unconscious of every thing relating to them ;
or in other words, he has no recollection of any such
consciousness. They have this peculiarity, that when
he has ended his sermon, he gives notice to his supposed audience, that the next meeting, for the special
purpose he assigns, will be held at a particular hour
of a day which he mentions. He is never troubled
with a fit until the proposed time arrives. He never
fails to observe his own adjournments, and always
with the utmost punctuality. The periods of his paroxysm are regulated by his own prescription at a
preceding meeting. Always before the dismissal, he
announces the time of the future meeting. He has
been under this diseased habit for several years, and
is in other respects well. His place of performance
is the upper window of his house.

A man not attached to any religious society, had serious meditations of his own. When volition was lost and consciousness suspended by sleep, he performed the exercises of prayer to God and exhortation to men with zeal and fervour. The paroxysm was renewed nightly; the time a little after he fell asleep; the attitude, that of kneeling in his bed. He knows nothing of these transactions but by information from those who have attended him. Being rather unrestrained in his religious opinions, he owns himself afflicted and ashamed on being told that he has become a preacher in his sleep.

During a calamitous war, a farmer buried some pieces of gold in his field. He forgot the spot, and sought his hidden treasure, until he despaired of success. The loss dwelt upon his mind night and day, and gave him perpetual uneasiness. At length, about fifteen years after the concealment of the money, he rose at night from his bed in a fit of somnambulism, and went forth to the field. In a short time he returned with the guineas in his hand. Being observed to be in a sleep-walking condition, he was waked by his wife and brought to his senses. His surprise was extreme on discovering his situation. And he immediately related to her and the family the dream by which he was instructed where to find the precious metal, which he produced in proof of the correctness of his recollection during that dream.

A boy very much exercised by somnambulism, fell asleep one day in the religious meeting he was attending. During that sleep, his somnambulism invaded him. It continued through the rising of the meeting, and during his walk to his lodgings. He then ate his dinner, went to school (it was a week day) and performed several tasks in calculation. After he done these and various other things, he suddenly applied his hand to his forehead, rubbed his eyes and waked up. He instantly enquired if the meeting was dismissed, and said he was ashamed of having fallen asleep. He had a belief that he was yet in the meeting; and had lost all recollection of events from the moment of falling asleep until the instant of coming to himself in the school. He had no recollection whatever of taking food, walking and talking, or of making calculations in Arithmetic.

I know a man who is addicted to talking in his sleep. His conversation generally turns upon the business he follows. He rattles on and discourses without the smallest reserve. The fit commonly takes him in bed. Whenever his wife finds the so-liloquy troublesome, she speaks loud to him, shakes him and wakes him. Then he ceases to speak, and once more goes quietly to sleep. If, on the contrary, the lady wishes to hear him further, she asks him questions in a gentle tone, and he discloses to her overy thing he knows. He has not the faintest re-collection afterwards of any thing he has said.

It would be easy for one to write more of these living occurrences by way of elucidation. Abundance of them are extant, offering themselves to him who will gather and record them. While they convince us that we have much to learn on the intricate subject of the mind, they assure us too that we have made important advances into this department of knowledge. The examples adduced are sufficient to illustrate the two conditions of the sensorium, first, when the images excited are those of the memory chiefly; and secondly, when in addition thereto, there is a degree of hallucination.

Miss B's case, combines the strong ideas of memory, with probably stronger hallucinations, especially of the organ of sight. This sense more than any other, is active in dreaming. Hence it has happened that extatic emotions, mental abstractions, trances, and a configuration of the sentient extremities, of the optical nerves from external causes, similar to that configuration usually induced by external agents, have been denominated visions. They are so called because the eyes are peculiarly concerned. Visions are usually accompanied with a belief of their own reality, on the part of the person who experiences them. But the bye-standers are frequently unconvinced ; or are perfectly satisfied that the objects alleged to be seen are not realities. And this makes the difference between hallucination or an honest mistake grounded on hallucination ; and imposture, or a contrivance deceitfully represented as true.

The case of Mr. Nicolai of Berlin, is a remarkable instance of hallucination in the organs of sight begetting phantasms which he knew to be illusions and which he could distinguish from realities by his own judgment whenever they appeared in vision before him.

The particular condition of the memory deserves to be noticed. In some instances, all that is thus seen is remembered: In others, the memory fails to record the ideas which for a season occupied the sensorium. In the present case, as in many that are analagous to it, there is a most remarkable display of memory, but a total oblivion afterwards, that there had even been such employment of the memory. The whole performance is like a transaction forgotten, or an image totally effaced.

I am perfectly clear what course of remedies ought to be prescribed. But on the practical part of this subject, novelties present themselves with a discouraging, a forbidding attitude. I have heard a sentiment from worthy people that it would be a pity to cure, what they term, such a divine disease. They are persuaded that forbearance ought to be shown to an infirmity, marked with what they fondly call, celestial symptoms. They caution me not to disturb the workings of a distemper, caused and hallowed as it were, by a kind and propitious influence. They urge impressively, the propriety of permitting the continuance of a malady, so physically and morally edifying. When, say they, the simple are instructed, and the wise are puzzled, by her discourses, medicine ought to withhold its helping hand. And why they cry, cannot the chiefs of the faculty, make a solemn pause when asked to cure a patient, whose voice in so peculiar a manner enforces the precepts of the scripture, bedews the cheeks of beauty with tears, and warns sinners to a speedy repentance?

New York, Nov. 10, 1814.

Prayer and Exhortation of one evening, as taken down in short hand at the time.

On the 16th of October, 1814, the editor was favoured by a highly respectable gentleman, with an opportunity of taking in short hand, the exercise which he now presents without either alteration or embellishment, in precisely the terms used when it was delivered.

Rachel Baker, retired to rest at nine o'clock, and scarcely had she laid down, when deep and apparently agonizing groans announced the approach of her nightly service, they lasted for two or three minutes, when with a distinct voice, and evidently with the most profound reverence and solemnity she commenced her

INTRODUCTORY PRAYER.

O God! I am sensible that I have come into thy presence, and have attempted to draw near thy throne of grace by prayer; be not thou angry with me O Lord, in attempting to call upon thy name, neither look according to my deserts; but be pleased to look upon the face of thine anointed, and for his sake forgive me my sins, smile upon him who is altogether lovely, and *I beseech of thee earnestly* forgive me my past sins, and forbid that I should have an unreconciled heart, that I should cease to reverence thee. O God, wilt thou be pleased to bow the gentle heavens, and condescend to come down and smile upon Zion, which

C

is now sat in a solitary place, coldness and stupidity seemeth to reside in the hearts of thy children, she is laid down by the cold streams of Babylon, and hangs her harp upon the willows, and seems not to recline so sweetly before the Lord as in days past; and wilt thou ride in the church on the wheels of thy gospel chariot, truly making the hearts of thy saints to rejoice, and bringing sinners to confess and forsake their sins. May thy children rejoice with joy unspeakable, because the day spring from on high hath visited their souls, and the day star arisen upon their hearts, because they are travelling to another world. Encourage thy children I beseech of thee, oh thou Father of truth, that thy name may be glorified here on earth ; and I would also pray that when I come before thee, thy kingdom may come. O Lord God Almighty, forsake not the earth, be pleased to draw near and smile upon the earth in mercy, that the land mourn no longer and lamentation be no longer known in the land, because thy judgments are so heavy, and because thou dost visit the inhabitants of the earth, yea! in thy judgment. If it can be consistent with thy will, in the midst of deserved judgment remember mercy. When shall the glorious time come when the kingdoms of this world shall become the kingdoms of our God and his Christ, whose kingdom is an everlasting kingdom, and his dominion forever and ever.

THE EXHORTATION.

Now, oh my beloved brothers and sisters, think it not strange that I call upon you to keep you in remembrance. Though I am but a youth, yet will I speak what the Lord shall say unto me, I exhort you my friends that truly you must continue in love. Let brotherly love continue, and abound ; exhort with a holy exhortation, so much the more as ye see the day approaching ; finally my friends may you be enabled truly to make sure work for your own souls' sake, may you cherish the spirit of the Lord when it is striving with you that you need not to grieve the holy spirit of the Lord. Consider how highly you are priviledged, for behold! we, even we, do dwell in a land of liberty, we can truly sit under our own vines and fig trees, and there is none to molest or to make us afraid, neither is there any to enquire why doest thou thus or so. We can hear the word preached in purity, we can be partakers of the fruit of God. What greater blessing can we desire than these! think of these and remember from whence they came. Behold the heathen, they do not enjoy these blessings, but alas they are putting their trust in gods which cannot save them; alas! alas! their gods cannot hear when they cry, nor when trouble overtaketh cannot save them : Our God is a God that can save us when trouble overtaketh us, if we meet with tribulation in this life, or temptation, the Lord will deliver us in due time. Even we that are professors, are truly compared to pilgrims and sojourners, although apt to meet with tribulation, yea, persecution, when we meet with these things let us not be discouraged or amazed ; for these are promised in the scripture, and you may know if you are christians by them ; for if any man will live godly in Christ Jesus he shall suffer persecution.

And the Lord hath said, "blessed are ye when all manner of evil is spoken about you falsely for my names' sake." I say unto you rejoice with joy unspeakable and full of glory; and again I say rejoice in the Lord, for he has laid up a crown of glory for you. O my friends, be not discouraged while travelling through this wilderness world, which is full of wickedness. Satan, yea satan, is suffered to go about in this lower earth, and it is of a truth that he goeth about like a roaring lion. He seeketh if haply he may devour. Yea, quickly he may devour us, even so it is with you, my friends, with the tender lambs, and sheep of Christ. If it were not for the good shepherd to guard his flock, satan, even satan, would devour us, and tear us in pieces long before this time.

But thanks be to my God, he is a good shepherd, he will not suffer any to pluck them out of his hand. And also, thanks be to my God, Jesus is speaking beautiful words to those that are weak, compared unto infants who desire the sincere milk of the word. O my dove that art in the Cliffs of the rock in the secret place of the stairs, let me see thy countenance, let me hear thy voice for sweet is thy voice, and thy countenance is comely.

Rejoice ye therefore O beloved friends, and again I say unto you rejoice! because Jesus our great shepherd has entered into the heavens and is pleading for us; and therefore "if any man sin we have an advocate with the father Jesus Christ the righteous;" rejoice therefore because you have a great high priest which is entered into the heaven of heavens and is there pleading for you.

Friends be not discouraged; it is but a little time to travel, shortly we shall bid farewell to earth; our bodies shall be numbered with the pale nation of the dead which is in the grave, and our souls return to our God. O my brethren and sisters. I beseech of you not to give place to the devil nor let the world ensnare you, fight the good fight of faith, run with patience the race set before you in the gospel, looking unto Jesus who is the author and will be the finisher of your faith.

How pleasant is religion! it maketh husbands and wives to live in unity, parents and children to live in unity, and when there is a family that loves our God, love reigneth, and may I be permitted to say, it is a little heaven here on earth. Grace maketh people to appear very beautiful. What is more delightful than to see young people in the bloom of their youth setting out to serve the Lord, nothing more delightful than to see these: but, alas! alas! when the youth say their comfort is in the ball chamber! amusing themselves with vanity, they are deceiving themselves, for no satisfaction, no real satisfaction can be enjoyed in these. Once I thought satisfaction was to be

taken there, but alas! alas! no satisfaction could be
obtained there; but alas, I, even I, when I was in
the ball chamber, was sensible there was a God, who
did truly see me. My mind struck me oftentimes
with dread, and fear, while going on in vanity, serv-
ing my master the devil; if God should smite me this
moment, and death should strike me, what should I
do? it would strike me so, that I, even I! could not
take satisfaction in the thing.

But thanks be to our God, through our Lord and
Saviour Jesus Christ, he has pleased to incline me to
run after him, drew me with the cords of his love
that I might be inclined to run after him. I, even I,
tell you of my former vanities, not that they are unto
me pleasing; but unto you, oh youth, I tell them,
that you may yet come and choose that comfort, that
will be substantial. Think not to say that I am deceiving you. I say, they that have the grace of God
in their hearts, they are the happy people, they be-
long to another and a better country, where pleasures
flow from the throne of God.

Be not discouraged O my Brethren and Sistens,
but pray for sinners; for when Zion travaileth, she
shall bring forth children to the praise of the Grace of
God; for this reason I would beseech of you to wake
out of stupidity. "Arise and put on your beautiful gar-
ment that you may appear bright as the sun, clear as
the moon, and terrible as an army with Banners."

O my friends may you therefore be faithful servants
of the Lord; that you may be of the happy number
that shall come out of the great tribulation, having
washed their robes and made them white in the blood
of the lamb. Angels and archangels, yea they do
dwell in the heavens above, they are clothed in daz_
zling light, so bright that mortals cannot look upon
them, nor carnal eye behold them; these beautiful be-
ings cease not at all, but do cast a glittering crown before our Father and are crying holy! holy! holy! Lord
God Almighty which was and is, and is to come, worthy is the lamb to receive everlasting praises from eve-

ry creature. Saints, yea saints, that have arrived there hundreds and thousands years ago, they have one continual song in praising God and are not wearied. The Patriarchs, prophets and apostles are there, they have long white robes presented to them and they have not changed their garments, but they are as beautiful as they were when they first put them on; they immediately joined the angels in heaven in praising God and have continued praising God to the present moment. Their clothes have not become motheaten for they appear dressed in fine linen white and clean. Saints that have died in the Lord's later years do join in praising God,

"All shining like the sun;
No less days, to sing God's praise,
Than when they first begun."

Jesus is the light of the city; there needeth no light of sun moon or stars; for Jesus is the light of the city; no, no night there, but all is day. Our Father he smileth upon his children, he biddeth them hearty welcome, beloved to live in heaven, let us follow on to please the Lord, by walking near him and obeying his commands. *Here there was an interruption by a question.* Rachel, do you think the people will believe you? *Ans.* Do I think the people will believe me when I speak the truth in Christ Jesus; I even I, do speak the truth; whether I do speak the truth or not, judge ye; better for them not to hear than not to believe; for there is a God to whom they are accountable for what they hear.

I know and am persuaded, my brothers and sisters will witness to the truth. Furthermore will I tell you, and leave you in the hands of the Lord, there is no other way; he hath said, I am the door, by me if any man enter in, he shall be saved, and shall go in and out, and find pasture. O, that the Lord our righteousness would help us his children to draw water out of the well of salvation, that our minds may be fed with the bread of life. Oh that the Lord would clothe us in the righteousness of Christ, that

we may be enabled to cleanse our hands from every
thing that appears like evil. I leave you in the
hands of the Lord, and when you pray, forget me
not; praying that I may be kept to the end, for the
prayer of the righteous availeth much. I will therefore turn my attention to poor sinners. *Here she was
interrupted by a second question.* Rachel! *Ans.* What
do you want my friend. Can you address the people
of New York, for you are in New York, and they
are now about you? *Answer,* I am at Scipio (the town
of her residence) and am talking to my brothers and
sisters, and repeated, I will therefore turn my attention to poor sinners, and in a few words exhort you
if haply I may be an instrument of turning them from
the evil of their ways. Sinners continue no longer
in sin, lay down the weapons of your rebellion, and
fly to Christ. Many times have I taken words and ex-
horted you. What, more sinners shall I say, shall I
spend this vile body of mine and you not hearken unto my voice? I, even I, would be willing to spend
this body, if I could be the instrument of turning one
soul unto the Lord, I perceive thy soul is worth more
than hundreds and thousands of worlds. What profit is unto a man if he should gain the whole world
and lose his own soul. What profit unto you to gain
this earth and lose your soul? we read the rich man
had the love of this earth and it bound him down to
the dark regions of endless wo. He lifted up his eyes
in hell, being in torment, he beheld Father Abraham
afar off with Lazarus, who was a beggar and would
have eaten the crumbs which fell from the rich man's
table, but now after death he was in glory, and the
rich man was in hell. This rich man was like unto
the fool who saith in his heart, there is no God. He
said no doubt, eat, drink and be merry, for I have
enough, and what careth I. He did truly make a
god of this world, but at last the grim messenger,
death, came and deprived him of this life, and he was
plunged into wo because he would not hearken to the
voice of our God. Will it not be more dreadful for

you in the day of judgment than for Sodom and Gomorrah? Will not you come and be partakers of the gospel feast? lay down the arms of rebellion and turn unto the Lord.

Dearly beloved friends, you are the beloved of my soul. As I do love my own soul, so I love you. Come, be partakers of riches, yea durable riches, and honour, and when I pray unto my Father, I will pray that he would direct me how to pray; for, if I should take words and not offer my heart, it will not profit me any thing. Therefore, I will desire to reverence my God, with my heart; also it becometh us to honour him with our hearts, that the words of our lips may be right before him; for our God will not be mocked by such things.

CONCLUDING PRAYER.

O! thou that dwellest in dazzling light and makest the throne above the place of thy rest, thou didst create all nature by the word of thy power. The heavens and the earth are the work of thy hands; the fishes that swim in the sea, the beasts that walk on the earth; the great waters and the dry land, also the creeping thing; and they ought to praise thee, yea they do seem to speak thy praise. The winged fowls do praise thee for thou art worthy; thou didst create the sun, moon, and stars, and they speak forth thy wisdom. Thou didst place them in their proper order, thou speakest unto them and they cease not to obey thee, thou didst create man out of the dust of the earth, thou breathedst into his nostrils the breath of life and man became a being a living soul, thou didst place him in a state where he could enjoy thee, but he fell, and by the fall of our forefather sin entered into the world, and if not for the sake of thy beloved son, we must have perished. Thou didst make thy son, to come into this world; he took upon him the pains of death for his children; thanks be to thy name that there is such a glorious way of salvation found out. Thou didst send him to open a way and a consistent way, whereby the children of men might come unto thee and be saved; help us thy professed children to believe, to repent of all our sins, so that our sins may be blotted out of the book of thy remembrance, that our names may be written afresh in the lamb's book of life; that we may have a right to the tree of life which is in the midst of the paradise of God.

Though thou art in heaven, and we on earth, condescend to visit us, speak peace unto our souls, give us of thy reconciled spirit, that we may be enabled to walk humbly with our God, while we dwell on earth. Clothe Zion with thy salvation that she may be able, to give glory to thy name. Wilt thou appear in behalf of thy disciples who are chosen to preach thy word, may they be men that lie low in the valley of humiliation, servants of the Lord, who shall preach Christ Jesus and him crucified. Raise faithful labourers and send them into thy harvest, for the harvest truly is great and labourers are few. Bless thy disciples who go into the dark caverns of the earth to preach the gospel to the heathen; where darkness is, may light break forth, where gross darkness is, may the sun of righteousness arise with healing under his wings. How long will it be. before the kingdoms of this world shall become the kingdoms of our God and of his Christ. whose kingdom is, an everlasting kingdom and all dominions shall serve and obey him. How long shall I cry unto thee, and pray that a reformation may take place on the earth? Help O God! for the goodly man ceaseth; for the faithful fall from among the children of men. Help! or we perish, for I am sensible and persuaded that vain is the help of man. Put it into the hearts of our enemies to return unto their own land in peace, put it into the hearts of this American nation to desire peace; I pray thee if it can be consistent with thy will that thy judgment may be removed. May thy kingdom come and thy will be done on earth as it is

D

done in heaven. May that happy era soon commence, when the knowledge of the glory of the Lord, shall cover the earth, as the waters cover the sea." When nations shall be born in a day, when they shall not need to say one to another know thou the Lord ; for all shall know him from the least to the greatest. Now be with ourselves, make them to be men of piety ! men, that shall seek of thee to instruct them in the wisdom that cometh from above, for thou hast said if any man lack wisdom let him ask of God, who giveth literally, and upbraideth not. May they be men, that shall be truly enabled to instruct the nation in thy fear. Come this way and bless us ; speak union betwixt us ! cause a reformation in our souls that we may rejoice in the Lord our Saviour and see good days :

Come holy spirit heavenly dove !
With all thy quickening pow'rs
Come shed abroad a Saviour's love,
And that will kindle ours.

Truly may the voice of young converts be heard here, in distress of mind for their sins. Be pleased to appear in behalf of my parents, may they come to the knowledge of the truth and be saved, that my parents and their effspring may appear before thy bar, blameless. Bless my friends and relations ; make them all to hear thy voice and live. Be thou a father to the fatherless, and the widow's God in thy holy habitation. Comfort mourners in Zion, reveal unto them thy son, who said, blessed are ye that mourn, for ye shall be comforted. Be with me while I continue on earth ; wilt thou forgive me my past sins. I am a youth given to vanity, forgive my past sins, keep me under the shadow of thy wings the remaining part of my days. Forbid that I should be left to myself, for if thou shouldst I shall bring a wound to thy cause. Be with me while I live, that I may do thy will on earth. These unmerited favours I intreat of thee for Christ's sake, to whom with the Father and Holy Ghost be honour and glory now and forever, Amen !

Questions put to RACHEL BAKER, *during her parox-*
ysms by different Clergymen at different times and
places ; with the answers she gave ; as nearly as
they could be expressed in writing. At these
queries and replies, many witnesses were present ;
and they all occurred in the city of New-York.

———◦::◦———

Question. Are you thirsty ? will you drink water ?
Answer. Yes ? but not for the water that man
drinketh, and thirsteth for again, but for the water of
life. I long to draw water out of the well of salvation.

Q. Are you hungry ? will you eat something.
A. Yes ? but I do not hunger for the bread which
perisheth, but for that which endureth unto everlasting life, which the son of man giveth.

Q. What is to become of the poor of this city,
during the inclemency of the ensuing winter ?
She sighed, and said :
A. That is a question too difficult for me to answer.
I have not the eye of God, to discern the wants of
the poor in this great city ; nor, the understanding of
the Almighty to devise means for their relief, nor the
power of God to apply it. But, one thing I know,
that God will provide for his own. He has said,
bread shall be given them, and water shall be made
sure : and, in regard to others, his general providence
will supply them, for he is good and kind even to
the evil and unthankful, he maketh his sun to rise
upon the evil and the good, he sendeth rain upon the
just and the unjust. He openeth his hand and satis-
fieth the desire of every living thing.

Q. What ought to be the conduct of christians
during the present war ?
A. They ought to pray, acknowledging their own
sins, and the sins of those among whom they dwell,
which are the cause of the judgments we suffer. Sin
abounds in our land, and God has said, shall not my

soul be avenged on such a nation as this ! They ought to pray, spare thy people, and give not thy heritage to reproach ; and, that in wrath, he would remember mercy, and remove present judgments, by restoring to us the blessing of peace. But I would warn you all, that there is another war, and a captain, who is never defeated, even Jesus Christ, who makes war upon sin from generation to generation. He is always victorious. All his enemies shall be defeated and scattered. For lo ! thine enemies, O Lord, thine enemies shall perish. O ye sons and daughters of men, I intreat you to enlist under the banners of the captain of salvation, that you may be saved.

Q. You have been to Dr. Mason's church this evening, and heard him preach, he is come to see you ?

A. I did not observe any of the ambassadors of Christ in the assembly, but I know the preacher has been with my God, and that my God has been with him, for I heard the truth. The grand theme of a minister should ever be Christ and him crucified. Ministers should be examples to the flock and in every good word and work, and keep low in the valley of humiliation. They should warn unbelievers, who are blind to the things of God. for it is written, eye hath not seen, nor ear heard. neither have entered into the heart of man, the things which God hath prepared for them that love him.

Q. By what means can the heart of an obdurate, rebellious sinner be changed, so as to yield a cheerful obedience to the will of God ?

A. Nothing, my friend, short of the almighty power of God, can change the heart of a sinner ; for, such is the deceitfulness and desperate wickedness of the heart of man by nature, that he would forever remain an enemy to God in his mind, by wickedness, unless God should make his word like a fire and a hammer, to melt and break his rocky heart in pieces. To take away the heart of stone, is the work of God, and the new heart is the gift of his sovereign grace.

Thus saith the Lord, a new heart also will I give you, and a new spirit will I put within you ; and I will take away the stony heart out of your flesh. O my fellow-sinners, unless you experience this divine change, you are undone, and must perish forever ; verily, verily, I say unto you, except a man be born again, he cannot see the kingdom of God: Are you astonished at this declaration ? Do you ask, how can these things be ? Marvel not that I say unto you, ye must be born again.

Q. Why does the Lord visit his people with affliction ?

A. The Lord afflicts his people for the same reason that an affectionate parent chastises a beloved child. Parents correct their children because they have transgressed and been disobedient, and to prevent disobedience in future : so the Lord chastiseth his people with the rod of affliction for their sins and offences, that they may be brought to repentance, and live in future more to his glory. O ye children of God, the trials and afflictions you experience in this world, are sent by your heavenly father, in love to your souls, that you may not be condemned with the world, and that you may be made partakers of his holiness ; for the scripture saith, whom the Lord loveth he chastiseth and scourgeth every son whom he reneweth. If ye endure chastening, God dealeth with you as with a son ; for what son is he, whom the Father chasteneth not ? but, if ye be without chastisement, whereof all are partakers, then are ye bastards and not sons.

Q. What is your greatest grief?

A. My greatest grief is, that the hand of the Lord is lying heavy upon me, and that he has made me to differ from my brethren and sisters in a strange and unaccountable manner ; also, that I am not sufficiently resigned to the will of my heavenly father in this my affliction, and I also grieve, because I do not live as near to God as I should.

Q. What dress do you like best?

A. And do you ask me, my friend, this question? I must tell you that I do not give myself to such vain things as only please the carnal heart. I am not anxious about the garments which cover my poor body; these garments soon grow old and wear out. But I desire to be clothed with my redeemer's righteousness. This is the dress which will be acceptable to God. I would advise you all to seek the garments which never go to decay; even to be clothed with the robe of Christ's righteousness; or you will not be able to abide the awful justice of the Almighty at the day of judgment.

Q. What would make you rich?

A. Nothing, nothing, but the grace of my Saviour. Silver and gold I seek not. I would give, also, the world and its possessions, if I had them, for the grace and love of, my God. The riches and wealth of this world are very pleasing to the carnal eye, but I perceive they are all unsatisfying, yea, like the chaff which the wind driveth away. O ye children of men, seek not the riches which please the carnal eye, but I, even I, exhort you to seek durable riches and righteousness, to lay up for yourselves treasures in heaven; to be rich in faith and good works; to seek the riches of the grace of God.

Q. Why do you exhort your fellow-sinners in this manner?

A. Do you ask me why I call on Zion to arise and shake herself from the dust, and put on her beautiful garments? because it is the will of my God that I should. If it were not, my carnal heart would never permit me to undertake it. It is according "to that prophecy, and it shall come to pass in the last days, saith God, I will pour out of my spirit upon all flesh, and your sons and your daughters shall prophecy, and your young men shall see visions, and your old men shall dream dreams, and on my servants, and on my handmadens I will pour out in those days, of my spirit and they shall prophesy.

Q. Have you reason to believe that you have an interest in this Jesus of whom you have just been speaking?

A. I must acknowledge I have many doubts and fears. When I view the unholy exercises of my sinful heart, when I see my short comings in duty, my want of sufficient love to God, neglect, of religious duties, and murmurings against the dealings of Providence towards me, I am sometimes led to doubt whether I have any interest in the redemption of Christ. But, at other times, when I remember, that, if I had never received divine grace, I should not love God at all, I should not grieve that I love him so little, I should not mourn for my iniquities and short-comings in duty. I am constrained to say, that I have a hope of an interest in Jesus.

Description of this young woman, and her exercises by an intelligent gentleman, at Cayuga, in March 1814,

————◦::◦————

I went last evening with our friends S. and H. to hear the famous female somniloquist, or sleep-talker, of whom I said something in my last.   We went at an early hour, that we might have an opportunity of conversing with her while waking, and of laying in stores for scepticism ! she is a plump, hale country lass of nineteen, rather above the middle size ; of a smooth, equal, vacant tranquility of visage, without mental vivacity or vigor.   You would pronounce her eye to be good ; but it is unsteady, wild and capricious, with an unusual, if you please say sickly, dilation of the pupil.   She is taciturn and diffident, with a heavy, languid drawl of utterance, which pains you.

Our conversation was of a critical cast ; run mostly upon facts relating to herself ; her parentage, nativity, age, education, health, accidents, religion, &c. and the amazing unconscious faculty of talking in her sleep.   She followed all our questions in a regular pace, she anticipated nothing, but on the last head spoke with reluctance, and in a manner which betrayed a deep sensibility of her misfortune.   It was not a reluctance called in to resist our incivility ; it was female delicacy, busy in secreting a deformity.

She informed us that she had been in this way about two years, and was not sensible of any bodily disorder which should occasion it.   She is of the baptist sect, and for many years has been a zealous and fervent devotee, and when sleeping, her mind, taking the pious tendency of her waking hours, appears to be wholly occupied with subjects of religion.

On this head she appears to be intuitively prepared to meet questions the most dark and obstruse.   She answers with promptness, with multifarious remark, right onward, without repetition, to a total exhaustion of her subject, and not unfrequently of herself.   These facts, the people with whom she lived, and who had been acquainted with her from her infancy, united in confirming,   The object of our visit being attained, and our curiosity more strongly excited, we retired to a neighbour's for an hour, and returned to full gratification.   She had been in bed some time, and in a few moments we heard her commence, the doors were

thrown open and we all entered.   It was a stormy inclement
night, and 30 or 40 auditors only attended, it was not uncommon, we were informed, for three or four hundred to be
present.

She opened with a prayer of half an hour, and delivered
herself with great distinctness, in a clear, harmonious, un-
hesitating and animated tone of voice, with much devotional
zeal and attracting fervour; when through, she sighed and
groaned as in bodily anguish for ten or twelve minutes, her
chest hove, she grated her teeth and catched her breath, as
one does with a palpitation of the heart.

At a proper interval, some one who belonged to the house,
calling her mildly by her name, observed that elder some-
body, his name I forget, had come some distance to see her.
On this, she laboured a moment as for breath, when she commenced, and went through with, a most elegant exhortation,
addressed to him personally, on the subject of his duties ;
urging him to diligence, assiduity and perseverance in his
calling, painting in colours of delirious ecstacy, the pleasures
of the life to come, for the life well spent ; and denouncing
in awful solemnity, with the shuddering terrors of eternal
damnation, the sentinel who slumbered or winked upon the
watch-tower, interlarding her discourse with many pertinent
scriptural allusions, and in a copiousness of language, which
indeed very much astonished us.   The elder in the mean
time,

"——— pale, amazed,
All gaze, all wonder———,"

Eying, in tremulous meekness, the oracular corpse which
lay before him, in deep, dead sleep, interwove the sentiments which dropt from it, with the awful mysteries of a
preternatural, "Saul! Saul! why persecutest thou me?"
and wept in silent obsequiousness.   In fact, the deep attention of the auditors, the sighs of the women, the pattern of
the hall, the howling of the tempest, united with the speaking corpse, as it appeared uttering its awful warnings to mor-
tality, offered one of those moments of retirement to the
soul, when we shudder and shiver in sublimity, like a cul-
prit at Rome, with his heels to the precipice ; indeed, I
was ten times within an ace of coiling up my logic and unit-
ing in the sympathies of the crowd.

Having finished her address to the elder, she
again into the same convulsions which she
interval, but visibly in greater pain

of an incubus; it was the last conscious grasp of life to its fixture; she was as colourless as dead.

This unexpected and frightful debility of the young lady excited our curiosity, and gave rise to a conversation with the lady of the house upon the subject. She told us that three nights before, the company had so multiplied questions upon her that she was driven to a state of the most alarming exhaustion, and whenever this happened it required six, eight, and sometimes ten days of kind attention, caution and forbearance to recruit her. We were very sorry for this information, as we were obliged to give over asking her many questions with which we had come prepared. The company on this information immediately broke up and we retired.

Now, friend William, what do you think of all this? get along 'as soon as possible with all your doubts; take it as a fact that it is no imposture; no delusion; and then let me hear from you.   [*N. Y. Columbian*]

THE END.

ts

y
h
.t
:-t
l,

)
t
l

od

Check Out More Titles From HardPress Classics Series In this collection we are offering thousands of classic and hard to find books. This series spans a vast array of subjects – so you are bound to find something of interest to enjoy reading and learning about.

Subjects:
Architecture
Art
Biography & Autobiography
Body, Mind &Spirit
Children & Young Adult
Dramas
Education
Fiction
History
Language Arts & Disciplines
Law
Literary Collections
Music
Poetry
Psychology
Science
…and many more.

Visit us at www.hardpress.net

Im The Story

personalised classic books

JANE IN WONDERLAND

LEWIS CARROLL

"Beautiful gift.. lovely finish.
My Niece loves it, so precious!"

Helen R Brumfieldon

⭐⭐⭐⭐⭐

UNIQUE GIFT

FOR KIDS, PARTNERS
AND FRIENDS

Timeless books such as:

Kids

Alice in Wonderland · The Jungle Book · The Wonderful Wizard of Oz
Peter and Wendy · Robin Hood · The Prince and The Pauper
The Railway Children · Treasure Island · A Christmas Carol

Adults

Romeo and Juliet · Dracula

Highly Customizable

Change Books Title

Replace Character's names with yours

Upload Photo/file inside page

Add Inscriptions

Visit
Im The Story .com
and order yours today!

9 780371 016619